BARRYSCOURT LECTURES

BARRYSCOURT LECTURE SERIES

Barryscourt Castle is a fine 16th-century
tower-house at Carrigtwohill, Co Cork.
The Barryscourt Trust was established in
1987 with the aim of conserving,
enhancing and developing the heritage
potential of the castle.

In 1996, the Barryscourt Trust
instituted a bi-annual series of lectures on
Medieval Ireland. These will deal with
aspects of medieval history, archaeology,
art and architecture, and will be
delivered by scholars specialising in the
period. The lectures will be published
individually and in compilation form.

Barryscourt Lectures I
BARRYSCOURT CASTLE
AND THE IRISH TOWER-HOUSE
Tadhg O'Keeffe

Published by the Barryscourt Trust
in association with Cork County Council
and Gandon Editions, Kinsale.

ISBN 0946641 82X

Publication of this inaugural
lecture was sponsored by
Cork County Council.

Series Editor   Noel Jameson
Design   John O'Regan
                 (© Gandon, 1997)
Production   Nicola Dearey, Gandon
Printing   Betaprint, Dublin
Distribution   Gandon, Kinsale

THE BARRYSCOURT TRUST
Barryscourt Castle
Carrigtwohill, Co Cork

BARRYSCOURT CASTLE
AND THE IRISH TOWER-HOUSE

Barryscourt Castle tower-house:
the north-east turret viewed from the Hall

THE BARRYSCOURT LECTURES I

Barryscourt Castle and the Irish Tower-House

Tadhg O'Keeffe

THE BARRYSCOURT TRUST
IN ASSOCIATION WITH CORK COUNTY COUNCIL AND GANDON EDITIONS

1 – View of Barryscourt Castle from the north-west
prior to restoration

THE TOWER-HOUSE IS THE LATE medieval Irish castle *par excellence*.[1] From the 1300s to the 1600s the great majority of Irish castles included, or were comprised solely of, tower-houses. What is perhaps most remarkable about the tower-house tradition is that by the end of the 15th century, all three populations in medieval Ireland – the Gaelic Irish, the English and the gaelicised English – had embraced it. This essay begins with an exploration of the beginnings of that tradition, before offering some reflections on Barryscourt Castle, and specifically on its main tower [1], which is one of the finest tower-houses in Ireland.[2]

The origins of the Irish tower-house: the topography of the medieval household, 1200-1500

The 14th-century flare-up of hostilities between the native and settler populations provides a historical context by which we might view the tower-house tradition, predominantly a feature of 15th and 16th-century Ireland, as detached from the Anglo-Norman castle-building tradition. Harold Leask offered an actual chronology: he argued that, following a whole century in which major building work had all but ceased, the tower-house phenomenon began with the early 15th-century offer of subsidies – generally £10 – to those in the Pale who were willing to build small towers to fortify their lands,[3] a scheme which reflects the failure of the earlier crown policy of ordering tenants to fortify lands or face confiscation.[4] The new orthodoxy in chronology, however, is that the tower-house first appeared not after 1420, but in the 14th century,[5] but no matter how narrow the chronological gap becomes, the tower-house still seems to be perceived in the literature as a phenomenon distinct from the Norman castle; the year 1300 forms an impenetrable *fin de siècle* barrier across which the Norman castle could not venture forward, nor the tower-house backwards. With little known about castle-building among the native Irish during the 13th century, the cross-cultural ubiquity of the tower-house seems to encourage the view that it would not have emerged without there first being a break in the earlier building tradition.

One can, however, see in the corpus of Norman castles sufficient architectural precedent, conceptual and physical, for the main elements of the later tower-house. Here we need to understand that castle architecture was, in general, driven less by the need to find the optimum military de-sign, and more by the need to function efficiently as the residence of a lord and of his household (those who perform 'private tasks at his expense'[6]), and as an environment which expressed his power publicly and within which he could administer that power.

The spatial relationships between public and private spaces within castles are exceedingly complex, but are central to understanding the architecture of the buildings. One might make a distinction between halls which were essentially public buildings – places from which affairs of the territory under the protection of the castle were administered – and those which were essentially domestic but which had the capacity to take guests on certain occasions. It is likely, however, that few Irish castles – among them Dublin Castle[7] – had halls which served exclusively public functions. Most Irish halls, whether free-standing or contained within ranges of buildings, are probably best regarded as essentially domestic structures.

In the early 13th century at Adare Castle, county Limerick [2A], the keep or donjon was placed within an inner courtyard, with a hall in an outer courtyard beside the gateway; in the late middle ages, a second, larg-er hall, complete with external pilasters and an entrance porch, was added within the courtyard. The keep presumably contained private apartments, and its placement in the inner enclosure suggests that the deeper into the castle precinct one ventured, the more private the space. The contrast between the horizontal axis of the hall and the vertical axis of the private space was consciously executed. Schemes not unlike that at Adare can also be seen in the 13th-century castles of Trim, county Meath, and at Nenagh, county Tipperary; the description of the 'castle and hall' of Carlow being so decayed in 1307 that nobody would rent them suggests a similar configuration.[8]

At Carlingford, county Louth [2C], a long rectangular building of

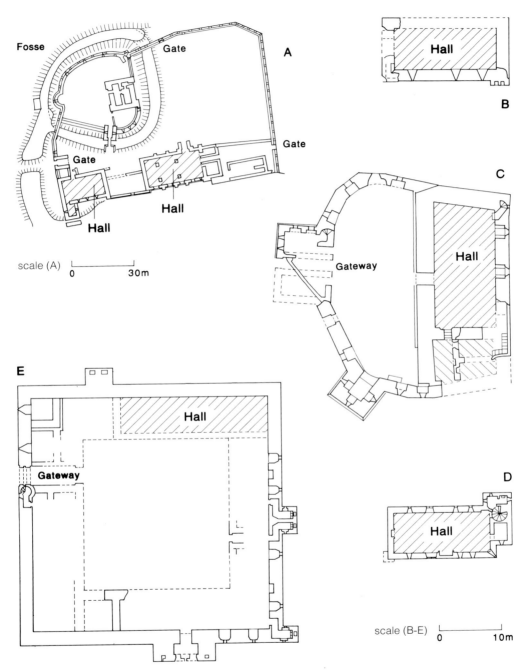

2 – Comparative castle plans:
Adare (A); Kindlestown (B); Carlingford (C); Coolhull (D); Ballymoon (E)

c1260, placed at the rear of a small courtyard of c1200, contained a first floor hall for most of its length, and the most private accommodation was placed not within a separate structure, but at one end of the hall. Ballymoon, county Carlow [2E], an enigmatic fortress dated by Leask to c1310, also has a long hall, and high-status residential space, marked by a projection containing a twinned garderobe, is attached to one end of it; unlike at Carlingford, the Ballymoon hall is fully integrated into a continuous range of buildings.

The domestic hall with the private residence attached to it, either above it or to one side, could be liberated from its setting alongside other buildings to stand freely within an enclosure. This is attested early in the 13th century;[9] it is apparently the case at the end of the 13th century at Rathumney, county Wexford and, in a slightly different configuration, at Kindlestown, county Wicklow [2B]. Coolhull, county Wexford [2D] is a 15th-century manifestation: here the private area is in tower form with a hall extending to one side of it.

Tower-houses such as Clara, county Kilkenny, and Roodstown, county Louth [3], one being a typical example of a southern and midland Irish tower-house and the other being typical of the Pale, differ from castles of Kindlestown or Coolhull type in shape: their axis is vertical rather than horizontal. A more fundamental difference is that in the tower-house, both the hall and the private rooms are made to conform to the shape of the building, so the difference in relative area between the hall and the private rooms lessens. In the case of Clara, the fourth-floor hall is still larger than other rooms within the tower, but is not as large as the hall in Coolhull. One can almost see the tower-house in embryo at Ballymoon: all of its rooms are of equal width, and even though they are arranged laterally rather than vertically, the castle's designer seems to be toying with the same concept of spatial regularity as informs the tower-houses.

If the strong vertical emphasis of the tower-house was inherited from the Norman keeps of the early 13th century, as seems likely, there are certain elements of tower-house architecture which are common to both keeps and free-standing halls of the 1200s. In the case of Clara, for example, the main stairs begins to the left of the main entrance, then rises uninterrupted to the fourth-floor hall, allowing one to move straight from the entrance to the hall without first entering a lesser room; the same arrangement is found in, for example, the early 13th-century cylindrical keep of Nenagh, county Tipperary (where the entrance is at first-floor level), and the early 13th-century hall of Grenan, county Kilkenny. Roodstown is considerably less complex than Clara, but here too the stairs is arranged so that one can ascend within the tower without first entering lower status rooms.

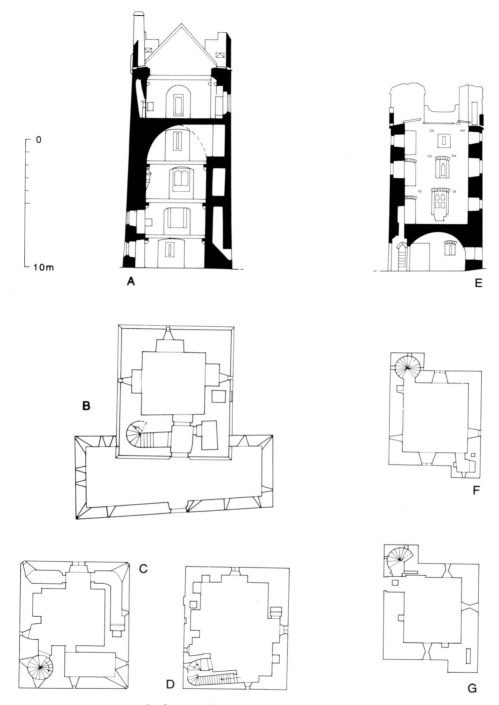

3 – Selected floor plans and cross-sections
Clara (A – Cross-section looking west; B – Ground-floor plan; C – Second-floor; D – Fourth-floor)
Roodstown (E – Cross-section looking east; F – First-floor plan; G – Ground-floor plan)

The continuity of architectural thinking between the 13th and 15th centuries is not surprising, but does it represent continuity in the social-histor-
ical contexts of the castles? Even within the colonial area, comparatively
few tower-house builders of the 14th and 15th centuries were descended
from the castle-owning population of pre-1300; instead, many of the
tower-houses may have belonged to those who had previously resided in
moated sites, monuments about which scholarship in Ireland was largely
ignorant until recent decades.[10] The moated site is the principal relic feature of Anglo-Norman rural settlement in midland and southern Ireland.
These sites were not castles in the sense in which that word was used by
contemporary society; rather, they were protected farmsteads, presumably
of manorial free tenants, and are generally unrecorded in historical
sources. Moated sites may have been built for the best part of a century,
beginning early in the 13th century, and most seem to have contained a
single house or hall, along with ancillary buildings. In central and north
Leinster, and in Ulster, moated sites are quite rare, and free tenants seem
to have perpetuated into the 13th century the tradition of building mottes.
Density maps of moated sites and tower-houses, based on the distributions
of rectangular earthwork enclosures and castles as marked on Ordnance
Survey maps,[11] show a general geographical correspondence [4], and one
might reasonably suggest that the tower-house, having become established
in the area where the moats indicate a strong Norman presence, spread
north-westwards into the Gaelic lands of Clare.[12] This is not to suggest

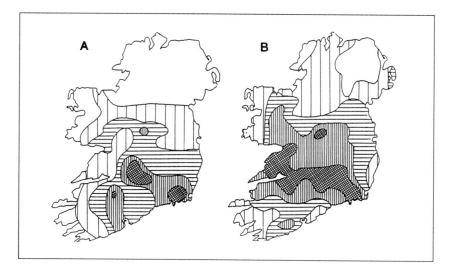

4 – Density maps of moated sites (A) and tower-houses (B)
the gradations are 2-10, 10-20, 20-30 and 30+ sites per 2500km²

that the tower-houses first appeared within moats, nor that they are architecturally related to the halls or houses within the moats, but it might safely be anticipated that future research on moat interiors will show the latter of these at least to be the case.

The Irish adoption of the tower-house is a most interesting phenomenon. Between the 12th and 14th centuries, their preferred forms of settlement and domestic architecture are largely unknown to us,[13] which is curious given the havoc the Gaelic Irish wreaked on the colony, both by territorial expansion and by cultural assimilation. The late middle ages would not have been first time that the medieval Gaelic Irish imported into their society a type of fortification which had originated elsewhere. One might think back to the pre-Norman 12th century. A consensus view of modern scholarship is that Ireland had already embraced feudalism by the time the Anglo-Norman conquest and settlement began in 1169.[14] Among the manifestations of this mode of social organisation in the early 1100s is the appearance in native sources of *caistél* or *caislén*.[15] Even more than the great cathedrals of Europe, whose construction in the high middle ages – 12th to 14th centuries – was made possible by the feudal organisation of contemporary society, it was the castle which embodied the concept of feudalism, and the use of this word in an Irish environment signposts a society conscious of the symbolism of language. The monuments themselves are unknown to us since none survives, but evidence which is largely circumstantial strongly indicates that for these castles, Irish kings, whom we know to have been embracing the pan-European Romanesque style for churches under their patronage, adapted the elevated settlement earthwork or motte, a monument then current in England and Continental Europe.[16]

The adoption of the tower-house by the Irish does not, however, represent an anglicisation of Gaelic society, even though the tower-houses which inspired imitation were environments designed and equipped for the domestic rituals of colonial society. Henry Chrysted tells us that Ó Néill, Mac Murchada, Ó Briain and Ó Conchobhair adopted only temporarily the manners and styles of the English court following their acceptance of knighthoods from Richard II.[17] Raymond, viscount of Perelhos and of Roda in Roussillon, encountered Ó Néill whilst journeying to St Patrick's Purgatory in 1397. Despite having an inquiring interest in overseas customs, Ó Néill informed Raymond that he regarded Gaelic Irish customs as 'the best and most perfect in the world'. Raymond observed a warrior society, living in poverty close to the cattle on which they depended; he noted that kings, bishops and others in the nobility went barelegged and barefoot, and that neither women nor men were unwilling to expose their private parts.[18]

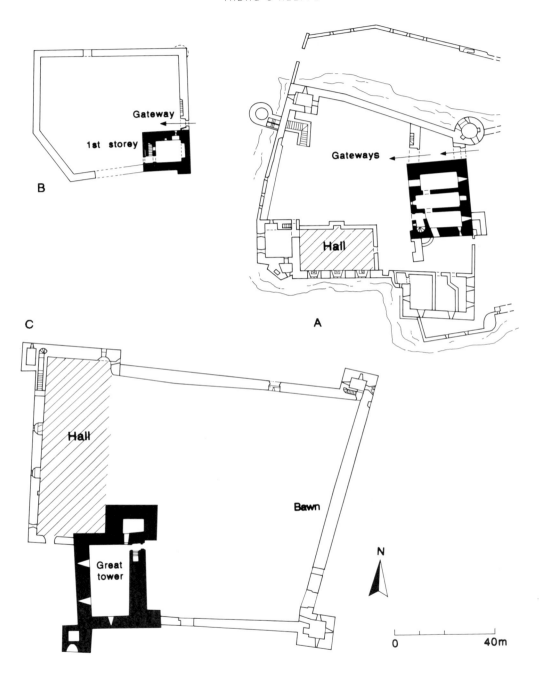

5 – Outline ground plans of Cahir Castle (A), Rathmacknee Castle (B),
Barryscourt Castle (C)

The tower-house of Barryscourt Castle: artefact, environment, symbol

Barryscourt Castle, or at least its tower-house, can certainly be considered from an architectural perspective to belong in the top rank of Irish late-medieval buildings.[19] Its layout adheres to a simple conception: the tower-house and adjacent structure, which can reasonably be identified as a hall, occupy one entire side of a quadrangular enclosure, with a curtain or bawn wall embracing a courtyard which extends eastwards of the two buildings. Both the tower-house and hall have turrets at their outermost corners, and these are mirrored in the small towers which protect, or at least define, the corners of the enclosure. The main entrance gateway into the courtyard – there is a second entrance in the north wall of the bawn – is overlooked by the tower-house [5C]. The plan type is not unusual: it is a variation on a theme which can be found at Cahir, county Tipperary, and Rathmacknee, county Wexford [5A, B].

A published survey of 1991 offers a detailed description of the buildings and a suggestion for the constructional sequence by which the castle arrived at its present configuration.[20] More recent survey work by the National Monuments and Properties Service of the Office of Public Works (now the Department of Arts, Culture and the Gaeltacht) has yielded a more accurate and comprehensive record of the remains, fulfiling

6 – View of Barryscourt Castle tower-house from the west
prior to restoration

the clear expectation of the compilers of the original report that the castle would continue to reveal its complexity.[21]

The tower-house, dating to c1550 on stylistic grounds, visually dominates both the castle and the landscape in which the castle is set [6]. It is our principal concern here, and a brief description of it, highlighting some of the evidence for substantial structural alterations to its original form, is necessary. Like many of the largest Irish tower-houses, its ground plan is comprised of a central block, at the corners of which are projecting turrets. The scheme is deployed here in a curiously asymmetrical manner: there are only three projecting turrets, leaving one of the corners (the north-west) unprotected. All three turrets are of different sizes, even the two which are diagonally opposite each other at the north-east and south-west corners, while the turret to the south-east is exceptional among the three in having one of its faces flush with the side wall of the main block.[22] The indifference to symmetry which is apparent in the ground plan, and indeed in the elevations, separates this castle from the likes of Bunratty, county Clare, where one can sense a progression towards the fully domestic house in which symmetry is part of the aesthetic. The Barryscourt tower-house is also rather squat in appearance, since its large central block, which rises to three storeys, has a lower parapet level than the turrets, each of which has five habitable storeys.

Entry into the tower is by a doorway – clearly inserted in the 16th century – at the north end of the east wall of the central block. Upon entering, a stairs rises to the left (the south side) while a doorway leads forward into the large apartment which is the lowest of the three floors. Narrow rectangular windows provided security for this large room, but at the cost of natural lighting. Only the large north-east turret has an accessible chamber at this lower-floor level, and this was reached from the main apartment through a door passage which was clearly mined out of the wall, whereas its original entry seems to have been through the floor of the chamber above. The main stairs rises southwards along the north side of the main block, terminating in a small lobby which opens into the main private hall at second-floor level. Halfway along the ascending stairs is a doorway, apparently an insertion, leading into the large first-floor apartment. This is roofed by a round barrel vault, which in turn provides the stone floor to the hall above, while a wooden floor separates it from the apartment below. The present vault is clearly a replacement of an earlier, pointed barrel vault, rough masonry traces of which still survive at the short ends of the hall [7]. The main first-floor apartment is no more effectively lit than that below, but it has a fireplace in its west wall which was inserted after the original vault had been replaced; a large circular patch of in-filled masonry located at the south end of the underside of the replacement vault may represent a cavity to allow smoke rise from a floor hearth,

7 – View of first floor room from the north showing traces of original vault

8 – The private hall: view from north prior to restoration

in which case the insertion of the fireplace is even later that the replacement of the vault. Narrow passages lead from the main apartment here into all three turrets. The south-west turret contains a long garderobe passage, but the south-east turret has a simple chamber which, in being L-shaped, exploits the thick wall of the central block. The north-eastern turret, however, has two floors at this level, both reached by ascending or descending flights of steps, which are in turn reached by a mural passageway between the turret and the main block. The upper floor has a small private chamber with a latrine outside its door at a slightly lower level. The lower-floor room has a musket loop overlooking the main entrance; it is set within an embrasure which was created by the blocking of a doorway. Also at the level of the lower of the two floors is a small mural chamber with a murder hole; this is contained within the thickness of the wall of the main block and directly above the entrance lobby.

The upper hall, a private hall, merits closer attention [8, 9]. Entered from the main stairs at the south end of the west wall, it was an elaborately appointed room, with five substantial, mullioned windows, one on the south wall and two on each of the side walls, providing abundant lighting. The northern window on the west wall bears the inscription DB ET ER ME FIERI FECER ADO 1586. A fireplace was inserted in front of, and thus blocking, the east-wall window, and is inscribed A D'O 1588 IHS DB ET ER ME FIERE FECERUT;[23] prior to this, heating was probably provided by a central hearth.[24] The hall originally had an open-timber roof supported principally on corbels along the side walls, and some medieval plaster survives on the walls beneath the line of corbels.

No less than six doorways open off the hall to provide access by corridors or by stairs to other rooms. Three doorways lead to stairs which ascend to give access to the upper chambers of the turrets and to parapet level. The stairs at the north end of the hall was reached by a long corridor, which also gave access to the castle's private chapel. The same stairs gives access to a passageway higher up, which leads towards the most important private chamber in the castle, located directly above the chapel and possessing a latrine (inserted), elaborate windows, all externally rebated and chamfered), and a fireplace inscribed with the legend A.D.O. 1596. Opposite the entrance to this chamber is a doorway-like opening in the end wall of the hall. An insertion of the late-16th century, it may have opened onto a landing or gallery over the hall, but is more likely to have provided the lord with a vantage point from which to view events in the hall below.

Three doorways lead from the hall to descending stairs, with two of these stairs giving access to chambers in the south-west and south-east turrets. The third – a broken doorway in front of the south window on the east wall – leads into a vaulted mural chamber which runs north-south

9 – The private hall: plan
SE   South-east turret
SW   South-west turret
NE   North-east turret
MC   Mural chamber
       (numbers refer to storey
       levels [see Fig.10])
Plan after R. Stapleton, Dept of Arts,
Culture and the Gaeltacht

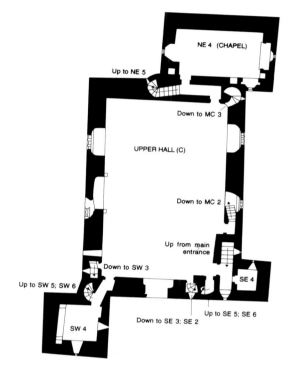

10 – A planning diagram of
Barryscourt tower-house.

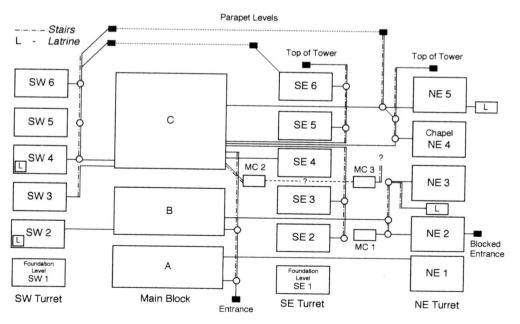

immediately above the main stairs. A wall seals this chamber at its north-ern end. Another stairs, now concealed in the north-east corner of the hall, descended into a similar mural passage at the same horizontal level further to the north along this side of the castle. These mural chambers are partly in-filled with rough masonry from the haunches of the present vault over the first floor, which suggests that they belong in the primary phase of the tower-house and were abandoned when the new vault was built.

There was no continuous access around the tower at parapet level. The ascending stairs in the south-west corner led to doorways opening onto the south and west parapets, but the former, wedged behind the bat-tlements and in front of the gable of the hall below, terminated at the south-east turret, while movement along the latter was encumbered by the chimney of the fireplace inserted in the hall below.

Lines of communication within the tower-house are complex, and routes between parts of the building were far more circuitous than might be expected in a tower-house. This is ostensibly a consequence of differ-ences between the heights of the main apartments and of the chambers within the turrets, and also of variations in the number and sizes of habit-able spaces within the tower-house. But the complexity of the pattern of access reflects more specifically the stratification within the household: not all rooms were of equal status, and the corridors and stairs expressed this by facilitating certain movements within the building, while making difficult or inconvenient the movements between other rooms by effec-tively increasing the distance between them. Some impression of this complexity can be given by translating the design of the Barryscourt tower-house into a planning diagram[25] [10] in which the main spaces with-in the tower are indicated by rectangular boxes of approximate propor-tions; horizontal bars represent corridors (lines of lateral movement within the tower), and vertical bars represent stairs (lines of vertical movement). Junctions – points at which the traveller through the building faces a choice between entering a space or continuing along a horizontal or verti-cal line – are represented by small circles. Other lines cross each other in the diagram, but no spatial or access relationships between them can be inferred; rather, such lines are a natural by-product of attempting to depict complex movement patterns within a building of Barryscourt's ground plan.

The planning diagram represents the tower-house in its final, pre-sent form. It is clear how much of the accommodation within the tower-house was accessible only through the hall (C): rooms SW 3-6, SE 2-6, and NE 4-5, MC2 and presumably also MC3, and the parapets, could only be reached by first entering this hall. Thus it acts as a form of courtyard around which other rooms are positioned, taking into its embrace not only those rooms which rise higher in the castle than it, but also rooms which are below it in the south-east and south-west turrets. The main stairs in

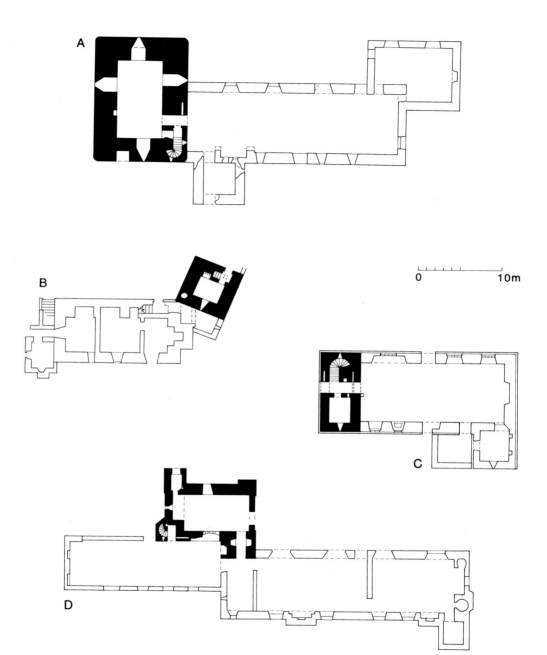

11 – Comparative tower and hall / house plans
Loughmoe, county Tipperary (A); Slade, county Wexford (B);
Lemanagh, county Clare (C); Athlumney, county Meath (D)

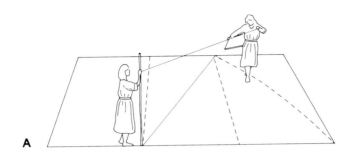

A

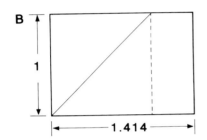

B

1

1.414

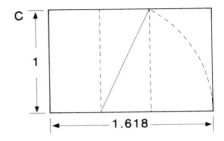

C

1

1.618

D

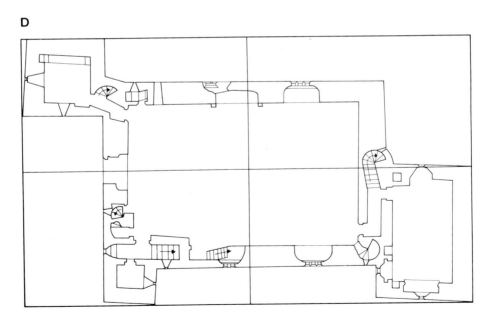

12 – The laying-out of proportional rectangles (A-C);
the Golden Section applied to Barryscourt tower-house (D)

the west wall of the castle ensured that one could enter the tower-house and ascend to the hall without having first to pass through any other room, but most of the other rooms in the tower-house were inaccessible without first entering the hall.

Given the evidence of alteration already been outlined above – evidence which has been forged into a comprehensive sequencing[26] – one might ask how the tower-house functioned originally. Before addressing this question, it is appropriate to consider the spatial and chronological relationship between the tower-house and the adjacent external hall to its north [5C].

———

In the majority of Irish instances where one has the tower and adjacent hall in the manner seen at Barryscourt, usually the latter is a later addition, often of the early post-medieval period [11]. The suggestion has been made that at Barryscourt, the hall is earlier, and that it has an even earlier foundation beneath it.[27] The fabric evidence for the present hall being early is far from unequivocal; certainly it follows a plan scheme which was used in the 13th century, with its projecting latrine at one end, and the external rebating and chamfering on its partially rebuilt windows is an embellishment which enjoyed particular vogue in the 13th century. But evidence which most firmly places the hall's construction *after* that of the tower relates to the method by which the tower itself was laid out.

The process of building in the middle ages was not based on *ad hoc* judgements of the relative proportions appropriate to the structure in question, but on tried and trusted proportional schemata of considerable antiquity, principal among them being those expressed by the ratios 1:1.4142 (or 1:$\sqrt{2}$) and 1:1.618 (the Golden Section).[28] These are mathematical expressions of long-used practical processes of laying out rectangles. Both involved the laying out of a square on the ground, marking the diagonal of the whole square or of half of it with a length of rope, then swinging the rope until it lined up with the side of the square [12A-C]. Medieval masons did not necessarily need to know the mathematics of their creation – that they were, in other words, expressing geometrically irrational numerical proportions – but the evidence of large buildings suggests they were knowledgeable about the whole number ratios approximating to 1:$\sqrt{2}$, the Golden Section and other ratios.[29] Acknowledging that masons possessed a knowledge of mathematics frees us to undertake metrical analysis; but it also contains the potential to create rather than recover schemata: plans may be analysed to reveal depths of mathematical consistency which were unknown to the masons but which were by-products of the simpler schemata.

The external hall at Barryscourt follows a simple ratio of 1:3, but the tower was apparently laid out within a Golden Section rectangle: the entire structure can be inscribed within a rectangle whose length is 1.618 times the width, with the width (east-west) of the north-east turret taking up half the width of the rectangle [12D] . The revelation is significant. Firstly, it helps clarify the relationship between hall and tower: given that this system was probably laid out on the ground rather than calculated, it is improbable that the latter could have been laid out to this proportional scheme so effectively had a hall already been standing to the north-west. Secondly, it suggests that tower-houses, like earlier Norman castles,[30] were laid out using sophisticated systems, and were not incidentally planned.

———

Returning to the tower-house itself, there are many indications that, notwithstanding the proportional system used in it, the tower-house is not the product of a single campaign of building, no matter how prolonged. Some observations regarding sequence might be offered here, but with the concession that on-going examination of the fabric may necessitate a revision in the suggested sequence. First of all, the evidence of an original pointed vault above the first-floor apartment is incontrovertible. Its collapse, probably very early in the tower-house's history, meant a new vault was needed, and the builders appear to have decided that a round barrel was more secure. Were substantial alterations made to the lay-out of the castle's interior at this point?

Two principal observations throw light on this issue. The first concerns mural chambers MC2 and MC3 [10]. The pointed vault had haunches wide enough to facilitate these chambers, but both of these were partially in-filled with the rubble haunches of the round vault when it was built, and the stairs connected to MC3 was abandoned. Where did this stairs lead? There is no evidence that it opened onto the hall, at least not directly. It may have opened onto the corridor which now leads to the chapel. Did it descend any lower than the mural chamber? There is no clear evidence that it did, and as the stairs leading to MC2 did not, so the same may be true here also. The second point relates to the main, mural stairs of the tower which runs directly beneath these mural chambers. That stairs begins its ascent at ground level in the entrance lobby, which is associated with the present ground floor doorway. That doorway is an insertion [13]. The tower may well have been entered originally at this point, but through an earlier doorway.

In favour of this suggestion is the stairs itself. It is not unknown for stairs to run along the entire length of a wall before turning into a spiral or exiting into a room.[31] Below the level of the entrance into first-floor level, the steps do seem to rise at a slightly different angle from those higher up, but this may not reflect a structural change but an error of judgement in the construction. There is certainly no reason to associate it with the inserted entrance doorway below: if the stairs had needed resetting because of a new doorway, one might find greater evidence of extensive rebuilding.

Alternatively, as has been suggested on the basis of an in-filled opening in the external wall of the tower,[32] the original entrance was half-way along the stairs as it ascended from ground level to the hall, with the entrance lobby here possibly extended northwards to what is now the mur-der hole chamber, MC1. Attractive though this suggestion is, it demands too many structural changes. It requires, first of all, that no steps descend-ed to ground-floor level: the steps would have to have stopped at the level of the mural entrance lobby. Secondly, that entrance lobby, as the vesti-bule serving the entire tower, would have needed to have been much wider than the stairs passage itself. It seems more likely that the infilled ope was a large window embrasure, and this would explain why it is not apparent on the exterior of the castle [13]. Also, it would be unusual to enter the tower at the level of the first-floor room but not be able to get direct access to it; the doorway which gives access to it from the main stairs is an insertion, albeit one which may pre-date the collapse of the vault.[33]

One might then hypothesise that the tower was indeed entered at

13 – View of lower exterior east wall of the tower-house
prior to restoration

ground level from the north end of its east wall, that the entrance lobby led directly into the ground floor, and that the stairs ascended to the hall *by-passing* the next floor level until, early in the tower's history, a doorway was broken into that first-floor room. How then did one enter that room originally? One possibility is that one descended into it from the hall via the stairs known to have been attached to MC2, but it is more likely perhaps that the blocked entrance at first-floor level in the north-east turret provided the direct access. The position of the castle's chapel may be pertinent here.

––––––

The layout of the tower-house reflected the social geography of the Barryscourt Castle community by creating linkages between some living spaces and by denying linkages between others. The elevations and details of the tower were no less expressive of the social order: the treatment of the tower's wall openings – windows and doors – varied according to the status of the room, or more particularly the status of the room's expected occupants. Those rooms given the most elaborate visual appearance will invariably be those with latrines or fireplaces. Thus the hierarchy or stratification within a household was encoded in a manner clearly legible to us.

The castle chapel, located within the north-east turret, was incorporated as was any other room in the access system within the tower-house, and like other rooms, its function was apparent from its furnishings: the sill of the east window, an elaborate double-cusped light set in a narrow vaulted embrasure, projected as an altar mensa, while a similar window in the south wall originally had a quatrefoil piscina in its sill.[34] A row of small holes about one metre above ground level runs along the plain north wall of the chapel, possibly marking the position of fixed stalls.

It may seem that this room could be placed anywhere within the tower provided the access was in keeping with the geography of the castle. But there were two pre-requisites for equipping the castle with a chapel. One was that the space be oriented east-west. The other was that it be located over an entrance.

Whether it was a feature of secular buildings prior to the Anglo-Norman arrival is unknown, but it is inherently likely that pre-Norman Irish kings had chapels within their fortresses, and that international architectural tradition – with which they were doubtless familiar – dictated that above the entrance was the proper place. The Normans certainly chose that position more often than not.[35] Trim Castle, county Meath, for example, has a chapel at second-floor level in the east turret of its keep, directly over the original entrance. Here the lord reached it from his private chamber above by descending one floor via a stair, a scheme similar to that at Barryscourt. The simpler scheme at Grenan also recalls Barryscourt: here a mural chapel is placed at one end of the upper hall, directly above the main entrance, and that hall, like at Barryscourt, was reached by a stairs ascending the length of the tower from a small entrance lobby.

If one accepts that the second floor of the north-east turret (NE2) was an entrance floor, then the chapel is indeed positioned above it, albeit separated by a domestic chamber (NE3). The south window with its piscina overlooked both this entrance and the present ground-floor entrance.

The widespread use in the middle ages of proportional schemata originally used in Antiquity may well have been intended to give buildings a classical imprimatur. It is difficult to imagine that the builders of Barryscourt were aware of, not to mention concerned with, the classical antiquity of their scheme, and to suggest otherwise might merit from the castle's builders a criticism rather like Turner's of Ruskin: 'he knows a great deal more about my paintings than I do, he puts things into my head and points out meanings I never intended.'[36] One could alternatively hold Schnaase's view that 'the retrospective view of the historian ... is fuller and richer than that which the contemporaries of past artists could have had.'[37] The Barryscourt builders certainly did conform to an iconographic motif of some antiquity in placing their chapel above the entrance to the tower-house, whether they were conscious or not of the iconographic meaning.

Epilogue

'We are come to the castle already. The castles are built very strong, and wth. narrow stayres, for security. The hall is the uppermost room, lett us go up, you shall not come downe agayne till tomorrow. The lady of the house meets you wth. her trayne. Salutations paste, you shall be presented wth. all the drinkes in the house, first the ordinary beare, then aqua vitae, then sacke, then olde-ale, the lady tastes it, you must not refuse it. The fyre is prepared in the middle of the hall, where you may sollace yor. selfe till supper time, you shall not want sacke and tobacco. By this time the table is spread and plentifully furnished wth. variety of meates, but ill-cooked and wthout sauce. When you come to yor. chamber, do not expect canopy and curtaines.'[38]

One can only guess that the reception which greeted Luke Gernon, a travelling Englishman in Ireland, when he called at a castle seeking hospitality in 1620 was typical of the age. Gernon's account of poorly cooked meat, straw-strewn floors, and a lady retiring early to her bed chamber, brings to life the reality of an evening in a well-to-do household at the end of the middle ages; it also suggests that the castles were less forbidding than the stark ruins might today suggest, and were instead places of rudimentary comfort at which strangers were sometimes made welcome.

By the time that Gernon was touring the country, the Irish castle was in the throes of its third and final morphological, functional and conceptual transformation. In the mid-17th century, the castle's incarnation as fundamentally a military establishment, or at least as part of the administrative apparatus of a militarised society, was several centuries in the past. Two centuries, perhaps three, before Gernon's visit, the greater number of castles were private fortresses, most of them possessing as a main element a tower-house. If these tower-houses contributed to a strategy of local or regional defence, that contribution was incidental to their primary roles as barriers against personal violence and theft. Within a century of Gernon, the domestic, entirely non-fortified house, was already in sight. If its emergence reflects a consciousness of contemporary English domestic architecture, or at least of such Irish manifestations of it as Carrick-on-Suir, county Tipperary, its actual realisation c1600 was facilitated largely by a social environment in which landed gentry perceived Ireland to be entering into a quiet phase of history. No less significant in effecting this radical change in architecture was the need to rethink defensive systems in an age in which gunpowder was commonplace. It is a curious irony of Gernon's account that by 1620, a castle like that into which he had welcomed – a type we know as a tower-house – would have been considered rather passé as a formal building type. The line of architectural evolution of the castle had, by that time, bifurcated: the private fortress was now a house furnished with timber floors throughout, well-lit windows, and exposed chimneys, and defended with narrow musket apertures, while star-shaped forts containing barracks buildings were entirely military in conception. Thus the concern of castle-builders, real or imagined by us, to reconcile the conflicting needs of defense and domesticity within a single building was finally resolved by a clear structural-functional polarisation.

———

The author

Tadhg O'Keeffe is a lecturer at the Department of Archaeology, University College Dublin. He is author of numerous articles on medieval Irish settlement and architecture, and his forthcoming book on Bridgetown Priory, county Cork – a study of the architecture of Augustinian Canons Regular in medieval Ireland – will be published by Cork County Council and Gandon Editions in June 1997.

Acknowledgements

It is a pleasure to acknowledge the Barryscourt Trust for inviting me to offer this contribution to the understanding of the castle. My thanks also to Noel Jamieson, Judith Monk and Red Tobin for sharing their views on the castle with me; to Richard Stapleton and Aighleann O'Shaughnessy for permission to make use of new survey material in figs. 9 and 12; to Margaret Coughlan for advice on the chapel and its context; and to Niamh Ó Broin for all the line drawings (except fig. 4). Finally, special acknowledgement is due to John Ludlow, whose initiative and energy have been central to the success of work at Barryscourt Castle.

Photographs – courtesy of the Department of Arts, Culture and the Gaeltacht

Drawings – by Niamh Ó Broin

Notes and References

1 HG Leask, *Irish Castles and Castellated Houses* (Revised ed., Dundalk, 1946), pp75-112; M Salter, *Castles and Stronghouses of Ireland* (Malvern, 1993) contains descriptions, plans and photographs. The outline plans of castles other than Barryscourt which have been used here are based on drawings in Leask and Salter; the Roodstown drawings are based on C Casey and A Rowan, *North Leinster* (Harmondsworth, 1993).

2 Barryscourt Castle is described and analysed in J Monk and R Tobin, *Barryscourt Castle: An Architectural Survey* (The Barryscourt Trust, 1991). More recent survey work has been carried out at the castle by Richard Stapleton, Department of Arts, Culture and the Gaeltacht, in the context of a programme of conservation and restoration.

3 Leask, *Irish Castles*, pp76-9

4 *Calendar of documents relating to Ireland..., 1171-[1307]*. Ed. HS Sweetman and GF Handcock. 5 vols. (PRO, London, 1875-86), 1171-1251, no.1576; *Cal Doc Irel* 1252-1284, no.411

5 TB Barry, 'The archaeology of the tower-house in late medieval Ireland' in H Anderson and J Wienberg (eds.), *The Study of Medieval Archaeology* (Stockholm, 1993), pp211-17; TE McNeill, 'The origins of tower-houses', *Archaeology Ireland*, 6, 1 (1992), pp13-14

6 G Duby (ed.), *A History of Private Life*. II *Revelations of the Medieval World* (Cambridge, Mass, 1988), p63; for a discussion of the medieval household see TE McNeill, *Castles* (London, 1992), pp47-72, K Mertres, *The English Noble Household, 1250-1600: Good Governance and Politic Rule* (Oxford, 1988), and M Thompson, *The Medieval Hall. The Basis of Secular Domestic Life, 600-1600 AD* (Aldershot, 1995), pp110-117.

7 In 1243 a hall here was built by order of Henry III. It was to be 120 feet long and 80 feet wide with glazed windows and a rose window, 30 feet in diameter, behind the dais. The king and queen were to be depicted on the same gable wall, and a great portal was to provide entrance to the hall. *Close rolls of the reign of Henry III, 1227-[1272]*. 14 vols. (PRO, London, 1892-1963) 1242-7, p23; see JB Maguire, 'Seventeenth century plans of Dublin Castle', *RSAI Jn.*, 104 (1974), 5-14

8 *Cal Doc Irel* 1302-7, no.617

9 Grenan, county Kilkenny, and Moylough, county Galway: McNeill, 'Origins of tower-houses', p14

10 G Hadden, 'Some earthworks in Co. Wexford,' *Cork Hist. Soc. Jn.*, lxix (1964), pp118-22; RE Glasscock, 'Moated sites and deserted boroughs and villages: two neglected aspects of Anglo-Norman settlement in Ireland', in N Stephens and R Glasscock (eds.), *Ir. Geog. Studies* (Belfast, 1970), pp162-8; TB Barry, *Moated Sites in south-east Ireland* (Oxford, 1977)

11 Glasscock, 'Moated Sites'; C. Ó Danachair, 'Irish tower houses and their regional distribution,', *Béaloideas* xlv-xlvii (1977-9), pp158-63

12 T O'Keeffe, 'Rural Settlement and Cultural Identity in Gaelic Ireland 1000-1500,' *Ruralia 1996, Památky archeologické – Supplementum 5* (Prague, 1996), pp142-53

13 Discussed in ibid.

14 D Ó Corráin, *Ireland before the Normans* (Dublin, 1972), is still the most valuable account

15 MT Flanagan, 'Irish and Anglo-Norman warfare in twelfth century Ireland' in T Bartlett and K Jeffrey (eds.), *A Military History of Ireland* (Cambridge, 1996), p61

16 R Higham and P Barker, *Timber Castles* (London, 1992), pp78-113; O'Keeffe, 'Gaelic Ireland 1000-1500'

17 J Watt, 'Gaelic polity and cultural identity' in A Cosgrove (ed), *A New History of Ireland*. II *Medieval Ireland 1169-1534* (Dublin, 1987), p350

18 JP Mahaffy, 'Two early tours in Ireland', *Hermathena* xviii, 40 (1914), pp3-9

[19] The castle's history has summarised in Monk and Tobin, *Barryscourt Castle*, pp4-7. The history of the Barry family is discussed by KW Nicholls, 'The development of lordship in county Cork, 1300-1600' in P O'Flanagan and CG Buttimer (eds.), *Cork History and Society* (Cork, 1993), pp178-81

[20] Monk and Tobin, *Barryscourt Castle*, pp51-64

[21] Monk and Tobin, *Barryscourt Castle*, 2

[22] Tower-houses with three corner towers or turrets are uncommon; parallels for the general conception of Barryscourt's ground plan can be found in the English Pale.

[23] DB and ER refer to David Barry and Ellen Roach respectively. David Barry died at Barryscourt in 1617 (Monk and Tobin, *Barryscourt Castle*, pp6-7)

[24] The south wall may have had a fireplace before the great window was inserted.

[25] The seminal work is PJ Falkiner, 'Castle planning in the 14th century', *Archaeol. Jn.* 120 (1963), pp215-35; G Fairclough, 'Meaningful constructions – spatial and functional analysis of medieval buildings', *Antiquity* 66 (1992), pp348-66

[26] Monk and Tobin, *Barryscourt Castle*

[27] Monk and Tobin, *Barryscourt Castle*, Fig. 4

[28] A useful summary is provided by N Coldstream, *Masons and Sculptors* (London, 1991), pp37-8; P Kidson, 'A metrological investigation', *Courtauld Warburg Inst. Jn.* 53 (1990), pp71-97

[29] For example, Salisbury Cathedral: P Kidson, 'The historical circumstances and the principles of the design' in T Cocke and P Kidson, *Salisbury Cathedral: Perspectives on the Architectural History* (London, 1993), pp35-91

[30] For example, TA Heslop, 'Orford castle, nostalgia and sophisticated living', *Architectural History* 34 (1991), pp36-58, and RA Stalley, 'The Anglo-Norman keep at Trim: its architectural implications', *Archaeology Ireland* 6, 4 (1992), 16-19

[31] This is the case in the early 13th-century hall at Grenan, county Kilkenny; the tower house of Carrigaphooca, county Cork, is not dissimilar; coincidentally perhaps it too was designed without wall fireplaces.

[32] Monk and Tobin, *Barryscourt Castle*, 30

[33] One cannot physically associate the re-vaulting of the first floor with the insertion of the doorway which gives access to it from the main stairs. Indeed, it is likely that the doorway is earlier than the new vault given that the room's fireplace may have been inserted before the vault collapsed.

[34] R Day, 'Notes from the Croker and Caulfield Manuscripts, etc, in Smith's History of Cork, with notes, *Cork Hist. Soc. Jn.*, 1A (1892), p144

[35] NJG Pounds, 'The chapel in the castle', *Fortress* 9 (1991), pp12-20

[36] B Cassidy (ed.), *Iconography at the Crossroads* (Princeton, 1993), p7

[37] M Podro, *The Critical Historians of Art* (New Haven, 1982), p33

[38] Leask, *Irish Castles*, pp91-2

THE BARRYSCOURT LECTURES

The Barryscourt Trust
presents a series of bi-annual lectures on Medieval Ireland
at Barryscourt Castle, Carrigtwohill, Co Cork

I

BARRYSCOURT CASTLE
AND THE IRISH TOWER-HOUSE

Dr Tadhg O'Keeffe
(Department of Archaeology, University College Dublin)

19 October 1996 (for publication: May 1997)
ISBN 0946641 82X

II

THE IMPACT OF THE ANGLO-NORMANS ON MUNSTER

AF O'Brien
(Department of History, University College Cork)

17 May 1997 (for publication: June 1997)
ISBN 0946641 838

III

TECHNOLOGICAL INNOVATION IN ANGLO-NORMAN MUNSTER

Dr Colin Rynne
(Curator of the Cork Butter Museum)

18 October 1997 (for publication: November 1997)
ISBN 0946641 846

For further details on the lecture series, contact:
The Barryscourt Trust, Barryscourt Castle, Carrigtwohill, Co Cork (tel 021-883864).

The Barryscourt lectures will be published individually,
and a clothbound compilation will be published at three-yearly intervals.
For further details on the publications, or to order copies, contact: Gandon Distribution
Oysterhaven, Kinsale, Co Cork (tel 021-770830 / fax 021-770755).